MASTERING YOUR TIME

I0482204

THE ART OF GETTING THINGS DONE QUICKLY AND EFFICIENTLY AND TAKING CONTROL OF YOUR LIFE

By

MOHAMMED KHAN

Copyright © 2016

Table of Contents

LEGAL NOTES

Copyright 2016 – All Rights Reserved – Mohammed Khan

ALL RIGHTS RESERVED. No part of this publication may be reproduced or transmitted in any form whatsoever, electronic, or mechanical, including photocopying, recording, or by any informational storage or retrieval system without express written, dated, and signed permission from the author.

DISCLAIMER: The information contained in this book, and its complementary bonuses, are meant to serve as a comprehensive collection of time-tested and proven strategies that the author of this book has applied to earn extra income. Summaries, strategies, tips and tricks are only recommendations by the author, and reading this book does not guarantee that one's results will exactly mirror the author's own results. The author of this book has made all reasonable efforts to provide current and accurate information for the readers of this book. The author will not be held liable for any unintentional errors or omissions that may be found.

The material in this book may include information, products, or services by third parties. Third Party materials comprise of the products and opinions expressed by their owners. As such, the author of this book does not assume responsibility or liability for any Third Party Material or opinions.

The publication of such Third Party materials does not constitute the author's guarantee of any information, instruction, opinion, products or services contained within the Third Party Material. Use of recommended Third Party Material does not guarantee that your results will mirror those of the author. Publication of such Third Party Material is simply a recommendation and expression of the author's own opinion of that material.

Great effort has been exerted to safeguard the accuracy of this writing. Opinions expressed in this book have been formulated as a result of both personal experience, as well as the experiences of others.

INTRODUCTION

In a world with smart phones, internet, and all the latest technology gadgets we have, you'd think that we have better time management. That's not necessarily the case. I bet that 80% of the people that are reading this probably spend countless hours just on social media. Refreshing the page, God knows how many times just to see if anything new is popping out.

I've seen more times than I can remember people mentioning to me that they don't have the time to go to the gym or go to this business conference, apparently because of some "exam" or because they have "work" to do

If there is one thing that I've seen the modern generation run short of, is time. Why does it always seem that there just isn't enough time in the 24 hours that God gifted us with. For some reason, just when we think we freed up enough time to do some leisure activity, something just has to come up.

I'll tell you, the answer to that isn't so complicated. People make things too complicated and that's where the problem lies. When you don't keep track of your time or schedule it properly, everything feels very very cluttered! And when things start getting cluttered, we feel like everything is just going to implode in our brain.

It all comes back down to the mindset. If you can master your mind, you can master your time. It's as simple as that. There's no sugarcoating it.

Now the real question is, how exactly do you program your mind so that you can take control of your time, which in turn is essentially taking control of your wealth, health and everything in between. Ever heard of the notion "Time is Money." Yeah I heard that too and as cliché as it sounds, there is some major truth to that.

For a start, you've certainly taken the first step in the right direction by purchasing this book. By the end of this book, if you've gotten anything out of this book, I would want it to be the ability to get MORE done in LESS time – provided you don't just work with effort and hard work but work SMART.

Chapter 1

BENEFITS OF EFFECTIVE TIME MANAGEMENT

Before we head on, you're probably asking yourselves "why should I manage my time." It's not like you need to manage your time, you've lived through your whole life without time management, and you're alive and well.

See this is the mentality that will constantly drag you back in to the ditch of no excellence. Yes you can live your life the way you're living it right now, but is that really what you want? Don't you want to excel in what you do? Don't you want to accomplish more in life? Since we're on the topic of life, lets also mention that we humans don't really live that long if you think about it. You go to school, straight off to work, a few years in retirement and that's it, then off to your graves. Is that really the life we all look for or want? If you ask me, I would rather die now than to live a life of no meaning.

Time management really does change perspective, it allows you the space and time to think and grow. To put it in simple terms, **time management benefits you in "all" areas of your life**.

I've never been one to take control of my time in most of my life. Lazy and procrastination would've been enough to describe the type of guy I was. And honestly, I don't mind. That laziness got me in some deep shit many times over. It took me a while to learn from my mistakes but I eventually got around to it. And when I did, life was very different. All of a sudden things seemed a lot brighter, I felt a lot happier. It's harder to explain than to actually experience it.

If you read in some of the benefits you will pinch yourself on how awesome managing your time can get. Here are some amazing benefits of effective time management.

Reduced Frustration

One of the lessons I've learned in life over and over again is to not do too many things at once. I come from a programming background and we are taught specifically to look at any situation from bottom up approach. When we look at any scenario, you want to start small and incrementally go up. That's how the world works and this approach makes it that much easier

When we don't manage our times effectively, we tend to clutter everything in our mind. This feels way too overwhelming and at some point, you're just going to explode. Many of the frustrating situations can be avoided with effective planning and organizing techniques. When you have overcome frustration, it is a lot easier to release the full power of your creativity and productivity.

You Will Be Happier and Healthier

Following a good time management routine will allow you to have more time to live a healthy lifestyle by sleeping well, eating right and exercising regularly. I remember one summer I would regularly go to bed around 4am and would wake up 12 hours later at 4pm. It was horrible I tell you. By the time I had woken up, half the day was gone. I felt too horrible to go the gym, I'd stay at home till it was time to go back to bed again. I'd flip through my phone, check my social media, watch some YouTube videos and end off with a movie. If you're reading this right now, you're probably feeling as icky as I am writing this. Gosh, I never want to go back to a time like that EVER again!

I can tell you, as dark as that time was, I feel a whole lot happier and healthier now.

You Will Have More Time to do What You Enjoy

This one is a no brainer. An effective time management routine will give you more time to pursue a hobby. Whether it's gardening, painting, hiking, sports or simply spending quality time with your family. Scheduling time for your hobbies and interests will greatly enhance the quality of your life

Less Wasted Time

When you know what you need to do, you waste less time in idle activities. Instead of wondering what you should be doing next, you can already be a step ahead of your work. I am a big believer in being aware of your situation. This includes everything and all things. A personal example is my finances. Not a dollar leaves my pocket or bank account except that I am aware of it. I track everything down. If I go buy a coffee at Starbucks, I jot that down. If I owe someone a few cents and pay that off, I jot that down.

This allows my consciousness to be aware of what I spend and how I spend. So every spending decision isn't biased, but well thought through. This is the same for time management. We only have 24 hours in a day. If we can take away 8 hours of sleep, we're left with 16 hours. Imagine if you had control over every free minute of your day and you were aware of it, how would you use it?

Increased Energy Levels

The undone things circulating in your mind cost you much more time and energy than the things you have done or are doing. It's as simple as that. And as I have mentioned previously, overwhelming your mind will not do any good to you. When you free your mind of unnecessary garbage, your energy level automatically spike.

Improves Your Reputation

This benefit is one of those less talked ones. The fact of the matter is, your time management reputation will always proceed you. When people think of you, they think of reliability. Your boss or your coworker isn't going to question you on whether you will get the work done on time or not. You're not going to have anyone micromanaging you, and I think everyone sort of needs that break anyways.

Road Trip Time?

The most wanted benefit of effective time management is the fact that you will have all the time in the world to do the things you love. Whether that's spending as much quality time with your family as you can, or traveling the world in short periods or one of my personal favorites, going on a road trip with your crew. I live in Canada and we have a whole lot of untraversed land. Periodically I'll wake up in the morning and as I've completed all my tasks way ahead of schedule, I'd call up some of my old friends and go on a road trip at the spur of the moment. I LOVE IT. Honestly, it's amazing how your life can be when you can free up so much time.

CHAPTER 2

7 MISTAKES THAT CAN DESTROY TIME MANAGEMENT

It wouldn't be a complete book without mentioning things that can hurt your time management really bad. Time management is an art, and with any art if things aren't done right, you won't reap the full benefits. As you're reading the list, keep these in mind and trust me when I say, I've fallen into some of these mistakes and the results can be devastating.

Failing to Keep a To-Do List

This one is really the tip of the iceberg, but a really big tip. Do you ever have that nagging feeling that you've forgotten to do an important piece of work? If so, you probably don't use a To-Do List to keep on top of things. (Or, if you do, you might not be using it effectively!)

In an age where almost everyone has at least a functioning smart phone, I don't know what excuse you could give me for not having a to-do list app.

Personally, for everyday tasks I use Google Keep to keep tab on my tasks. The reason why I stick with Googles app is because of its cloud infrastructure and its ability to synchronize between all your devices. It's also linked to your gmail account. I must admit that Google Keep has very basic functionality so you might want to check another app out with regards to something else like your day job or business for keeping tabs on your tasks.

Not Setting Personal Goals

Do you know where you'd like to be in six months? What about this time next year, or even 10 years from now? If not, it's time to set some personal goals!

Here's a vision test I'm constantly doing throughout my life and it hasn't failed me yet. Grab a pen and a piece of paper and start writing.

I like to envision myself in 6 months, 1 year, 2 years and 5 years. This will probably take at most 15 minutes of your time. For each phase, I write down all my goals that I'd like to accomplish. Take note that these goals must be as REALISTIC as they can be. I've set in the past goals that were far from my reach, and it left me kind of devastated for not achieving them. Who was I kidding, 1 million dollars in one year haha! Anyways you must judge your own abilities and situations.

I do this about once a month and it always gives me a fresh new sense of excitement and motivation.

Starting Your Day Late

If you study the success stories of successful people, one of the things they all have common is the habit of starting their day early, some extremely early. Richard Branson wakes up around 5:45 a.m. to do his daily exercise. Apple CEO, Tim Cook started his day at 4:30 a.m. and Procter & Gamble CEO, A.G. Lafley wakes up around 5:00–5:30 a.m and is at his desk by 6:30 a.m. or 7:00 a.m. at the latest.

I'm pretty sure you guys have already read the numerous benefits of waking up early and how it can have a positive impact on your life so I'm not going into that much detail here, but I can tell you how much of an impact it made in my life, my work and my business.

I've mentioned here before of my infamous sleeping schedule of sleeping around 4am (A time where Tim Cook is waking up) and waking up around 3-4 pm. I've come from a severe insomnia and it took me a while to break off the insomnia and get into normal sleeping habits. I took it a step further after reading about the amazing benefits of waking up early in the day.

I usually go to bed at 11pm and wake up around 6am. This gives me enough sleep time without the need of coffee. Before I go to bed, I'd write down a couple of prioritized tasks I'd like to get done by 8am. After waking up I usually stretch my hands as far as I can and do some light exercises. This gives me a boost of energy to do my tasks.

Aside from the health benefits of waking up early, I finish all my major tasks in the morning. This way after work, I have all the time in the world to do anything I want and not feel guilty about it.

I use to have really bad sleeping bags, those are about gone. I feel happier every single time I wake up early, knowing that most people are asleep so I could focus on my work without any distractions.

Not Prioritizing

Sometimes, it's hard to know how to prioritize, especially when you're facing a flood of seemingly-urgent tasks. However, it's essential to learn how to prioritize tasks effectively if you want to manage your time better.

Tasks with the highest priority will always be at the back of your head. They hold an immense amount of weight and the longer you hold on to them, the longer you will feel stressful.

Here's an exercise you can do. Take a piece of paper and write down all your tasks for the day. Once you have written all the tasks, number each one based on priority. The task with the most priority will have the number 1 beside it. Keep that piece of paper in handy as you will be looking back at it throughout the day. You don't necessarily have to use a piece of paper. Any note taking app on your smartphone would do also. Start doing your tasks based on that list of priority. It would be recommended to finish the tasks with the most priority in the morning which will leave a lot of room and time to finish of the rest of the tasks.

Failing To Manage Distractions

Did you know that on average, we humans lose about 2 hours a day to distractions? Outrageous I know! Now think of how much you could've done in those 2 hours, how much you could've done to make the world just a little bit better off.

If you want to gain control of your day and do your best work, it's vital to know how to **minimize distractions** effectively. For instance, turn off access to all your social media, or better yet, turn your cellphone on silent while doing a task. The point is to get the task done as efficiently as possible without losing any time. Your phone will probably add an hour to your task in the form of distraction.

Procrastination

I've been there, done that and let me tell you, that's not somewhere you want to be although I'm pretty sure you've also been there and done that. Procrastination occurs when you put off tasks that you should be focusing on right now. When you procrastinate, you feel guilty that you haven't started; you come to dread doing the task; and, eventually, everything catches up with you when you fail to complete the work on time.

One useful strategy that has been working well for me is to divide up a task and work on it incrementally. Often, procrastinators feel that they have to complete a task from start to finish, and this high expectation makes them feel overwhelmed and anxious. Instead, focus on devoting a small amount of time to starting. That's all!

If a task takes about an hour, divide it into two parts. Work on it for 30 minutes and then take a coffee break for about 15 minutes. Come back and finish the rest. That's all!

Taking On Too Much

I've done this over and over again in my life until I finally realized, UNDERSTAND YOUR LIMITS. When people are extremely motivated to do something, they just want to do it all. You have to understand that in the long run, your motivation will run out and you will completely burn yourself from exhaustion.

I currently run a blog (http://earnsixfigurenow.com), write kindle books like this one and have a drop-shipping business. Any more and I wouldn't be able to handle it. What I am doing now is maximizing my efforts into my current projects and once I am comfortable with it, I will then move on to other ventures. This goes for everything else. If you have 5 different projects due within 2 weeks, don't wait till the last day and submit half-assed work. Instead take about 3 days for each project. This way doing each project will be less of a burden and you can submit them with excellence. Isn't the point of working on our time management to exceed in our life with excellence?

CHAPTER 3

PLAN AHEAD AND INCREASE PRODUCTIVITY

For me, and probably for many of you as well, being able to accommodate work-life balance (including things like dieting, relaxation, and working out) is a serious challenge. It's not impossible, though…

The best point forward is **thinking in advance**. We've talked about this in the previous chapter on how not planning ahead can be a major no no in effective time management. In this chapter we'll be going through the nuts and bolts of it all. I'll be showing you **how to effectively plan your day** and improve your productivity.

Take about 10 minutes each evening (whenever you have some spare time) **and plan the next day.** You can use a simple tool like Google Calendar to schedule your workouts and activities. I personally use isoTimer. Alternatively you can use simple pen and paper if you're not so fond of smartphones or technology (hey I'm not judging). With isoTimer I can add notes, color coded tasks (so for example green for work related activities), add notes, set reminders and many more.

You need to know how much time you have in a given day and how much of it you will need to complete each activity. When you have jotted down an activity in the app, estimate how long it will take and set it to that amount.

The reason why I like doing this process every single day is the fact that you can see your day in a very visual way. You can see from a bird eye point of view where the gaps are for free time and what time you will be busy. This way if someone asks you if you're free at a certain time, you won't end up saying "I'll see, I might be busy."

Instead a more appropriate answer would be "Unfortunately, I won't be available at that time."

Here are the exact steps I take in my 10 minutes of glory to be as productive as I can the next day.

Color Code Your Tasks

If you're using an app (get one that has color coding option) or just writing with pen and paper, make sure to color code your tasks. For instance, if you have a task that is related to your work, then color it blue. If you have something for school, color it yellow and so on and so forth. This may be simple but I cannot begin to tell you how much of an impact it can make in your day to day schedule. In essence, it makes everything very neat, organized and decluttered.

Prioritize Your Tasks

It's important you determine which tasks are most important and should be done first and which can wait. You can write down your list of tasks in any simple note taking app (I use Google Keep) or on paper.

Some people find it very hard to prioritize tasks and can't for the love of God decide if one task is more important than the other. Seriously, just follow these guidelines.

- Which task is due first
- Which task will take the longest time to complete
- Which tasks are the most important, relative to their value
- Which task is the most challenging
- Which task will give you the quickest return on time investment

Once you've decided your priority list, mark each task down with either a number or letter in descending order. This helps you keep tab on your tasks so you don't lose focus on what to do next.

Once you've noted down the priority by number or letter, right below it make another note saying when this task should be done by.

Schedule a Time for Each Task

Write how long you expect to spend on each task. For example, you may have scheduled time in a given day to study (2 hours), workout (1 hour), write two emails (30 minutes), and walk the dog (30 minutes). It's key to allow you the necessary amount of time to complete each task; you'll only stress yourself out if you schedule yourself too tightly and aren't realistic about the amount of time things take.

Add Time Cushions To Your Schedule

What do I mean by this? Most people tend to underestimate the amount of time a certain task takes.   In most cases, you should overestimate how long a certain task takes. For instance, schedule something for 10 minutes which technically take 8 minutes to complete. These extra minutes will add up and provide a cushion which can help you avoid being late or falling behind. These cushions are used to make up for the time that is lost due to unexpected occurrences. For example, you might schedule your gym hour for 45 minutes but have to consider that it may take longer due to interactions with other people, time spent in the change room etc.

So for example… here's a visual look at all the steps combined

Red – School
Blue – Work

Work Total Allowable Hours (30 Minutes)

Process Store Orders (1)
- Due by the end of the day
- 7:30pm – 8pm - Today

School Total Allowable Hours (2.5 hours)

Assignment (2)
- Due by April 10th 2016
- 5pm – 5:30pm – Tomorrow

Essay (3)
- Due by April 13th 2016
- 7pm – 9pm – Tomorrow

Tasks are done. Now what?

Once you have completed your tasks, make sure to cross the tasks out. This has a very subtle physiological effect on us. It gives use the impression that we now have a lot less work to do. If you were to keep it uncrossed/unchecked, this would give an indication to our minds that we still have many tasks left. I know you've all had the feeling of being very overwhelmed at least once in your life. Let me tell you, that feeling is not good for the body or mind. So do what you can to get rid of that feeling.

Now comes the good part, you've done your tasks and are feeling pretty nice right about now. Go reward yourself. Take a hot bath, get a massage, watch your favorite TV show. I don't care. Do something to reward yourself. Trust me when I say, you will feel great and will want to come back and create a schedule for yourself every day. It's the motivation that comes with rewarding yourself that feels so great.

CHAPTER 4

8 WAYS TO ELIMINATE SOURCES OF DISTRACTION

Imagine you live in a small town, in the suburbs of a big city. You suddenly have to visit your sick parents who live in another small town near the outskirts of the city. The fastest way to get there is to take the highway. It will take you some time to get there as you live in the core of downtown but once you head to the ramp of the highway, you'll arrive there in no time.

Now imagine that for some unknown reason, the highway has a closure at the same time you leave your house. You're stuck taking the local roads. At first it doesn't seem so bad because the distance is shorter by about 25 miles. But once you start your journey, you realize there are a lot of stop signs, traffic lights, pedestrians and a whole bunch of other distractions which takes you twice as long to get to your destination.

This is no different than working on a group project or business. When you have distractions, you are possibly increasing your finish time by twice as much or even thrice as much.

Trying to work on a task while constantly getting interrupted from an endless amount of sources will dramatically increase the time it takes to finish that task.

You might tell yourself *"minor distractions aren't that bad are they?"*

Well I got bad news for you buddy, studies have shown that it takes on average 21 minutes to regain your focus after being interrupted.

"Simplicity is ultimately a matter of focus." — Ann Voskamp

To live life with less distraction, consider implementing one or more of these 10 distraction killing habits.

Put That Phone Away

Did you know that the average person in today's world checks their phone about 150 times a day. That's equivalent to about every 6 minutes. I know right, that's outrageous but the truth is, even I'm guilty of that.

It is important that you put your phone away in a different room. If that's too much of a stretch, put your phone on silent. No sound, no vibration! I know what you're thinking,

"What if I miss an important phone call or text?"

Chances are you won't. If you work uninterrupted for 40 minutes and take a 10-15 minute break, you can check your notifications then. But until then, it is crucial that you don't look at your phone even once.

Read or Answer Emails Only Twice a Day

When we keep our email client open all day, we tend to keep ourselves occupied with the most recent emails rather than the most important ones. If you look at what influential figures such as Michael Hyatt, or Scott Belsky have to say about checking and answering your emails, you will realize both recommend that you check and answer your emails only twice a day.

I usually dedicate about 15 each time. Once in the early morning after my morning routine which I will explain to you in a couple of chapters. And once in the evening when I have some free time.

Have Necessary Programs Ready before Starting the Task

What I mean by that is if you are working on your computer, don't open important files needed to complete the task while doing the task. Those few seconds you spend opening the files will cause unnecessary distraction and you can do without that.

Take a minute before you start to mentally walk yourself through what you need to do. This will help you gather your thoughts and see what files and programs you need in order to get the job done.

Remove Physical Clutter

Consider this: everything in our eyesight subtly pulls at our attention at least a little. When you clean up your clutter, you automatically have a fresh sense of purpose. Believe it or not, you will actually enjoy doing your work that much more. You will appreciate the minimalistic approach. Clutter messes with our minds, it holds us back and adds more to wasteful time.

Remove Virtual Clutter

This ones right up there with the physical clutter. We live in a time where most of our work is being done on our computers. Don't be one of those guys that has 20 tabs on Google Chrome on, 10 different applications as well as 7 different word files on. Along with that, the desktop screen has 100 applications.

Learn to organize your virtual settings. Put related applications in a folder. Delete the web browser tabs you don't need. Only keep the word files that are important open.

Once you declutter your virtual setting, you'll be surprised at your newfound ability to focus.

Establish a Morning Routine

The holy grail of distraction free setting is in the morning. No incoming emails, phone calls or people to bother you. Take a cold (or hot) shower. Drink your coffee or tea and fix yourself a warm breakfast.

Use Headphones

Often times, you will find yourself doing work in a very noisy environment. If there is nothing much you can do with regards to changing the environment, I suggest you get yourself a pair of headphones, and listen to soothing music or tone. If that is distracting to you as well, you can use the headphones for noise cancellation or play some white noise to cancel out the distractions.

Cancel Cable

If you haven't done this yet, I suggest you get to it! I've been cable free for about 6 years now and I cannot begin to tell you how much of an impact it has made thus far. According to some studies, humans on average spend about 9 years watching cable TV.

The problem with cable is it force feeds you into watching whatever they want to show you. This has a domino effect which in turn forces you to watch for several hours straight.

If you want to watch a certain movie, you can subscribe to Netflix or if you want to watch certain TV shows, you can subscribe to Hulu. Ultimately it is still cheaper than subscribing to cable television. And you are more selective with what you watch, which in turn reduces the amount of on screen time you watch.

CHAPTER 5

10 WAYS YOU'RE WASTING YOUR TIME AND HOW TO CHANGE IT

Everyone has 24 hours in a day. What you do with that time is totally up to you, but you may be wasting time throughout each day which can be holding you back from achieving other goals.

If you can pinpoint and figure out where exactly you waste your time, the possibilities are endless. You can start a side hustle, make more money and/or pay off your debt. You can learn new skills, spend quality time with family and friends, travel a lot more or just have fun in general.

Most people (and if you are most people) have what I call time leakage. Which essentially means there are points in our daily life where we do nothing proactive or beneficial in any way shape or form.

If you look at the bigger picture, ask yourself if you had an extra 5-10 hours per week, what could you do with that time?

Here are 10 ways you're wasting time and how to change that.

1 - Checking Your Email Constantly

This is a very common habit that people should stop right away. I'm not going to lie, I'm guilty of this as well, or at least I use to be. Now I actually time myself every single time I'm checking my email. I

dedicate about 15 minutes to checking my emails once every morning and once every night. That's it, nothing more.

The problem with constantly checking your email is it makes it easy to lose your train of thought when you should actually be doing something else.

2 - Multitasking

Some people can actually multitask pretty well but if you're the average human being, you should know our minds are not wired to take too many tasks at once. Switching back and forth between every task makes you lose focus, so each time you end up refocusing again which ultimately wastes more time.

Bottom line, **do one task at a time.** Don't start the next one till you finish the current one.

3 - Being Unorganized

Being unorganized can lead to many things such as more stress, lost items, late fees due to forgetting where things are, and much more.

Did you know…

- In a recent survey, 55% of consumers stated they would save anywhere from 16 to 60 minutes a day if they were organized.
- Every day the average office worker spends 1.5 hours looking for things.
- 23% of people pay bills late and have to pay late fees because they are unable to find their bills.
- The average person spends 12 days per year looking for things they can't find.

4 - Being Negative

You are wasting your time when you are being negative, literally. When I mean being negative, I mean having remorse, being regretful, feeling down, acting lazy, being mean or rude, you get the point.

When anyone is in a state of negativity, firstly nothing good comes out of it, and secondly **our mind cannot accept negativity and productivity together**, it simply cannot happen.

Try staying away from negativity, and find or do things that will make you happy. That should push off your negativity.

5 - Watching TV

The average person watches TV for over 35 hours per week! That is insane. 35 hours a week is full time work hours for some. If you really believe time is money, you just lost out on 35 hours of earning money.

I watch TV shows from time to time but when your life revolves around TV when you are bored, you really could use all those hours for something better like improving relations, or earning money.

Pro Tip: Get rid of your cable subscription and invest in either a Hulu subscription or Netflix.

6 - Spending Too Much Time on Social Media

Boy oh boy is this a big one. The amount of on screen time people waste on social media is ridiculous. A couple years ago we would've been good with just Facebook and Twitter. Now we have pinterest, snapchat, Instagram, and whole lot of other platforms.

With all these distractions, it can be pretty easy to waste away your day. I usually tell my clients the same thing I tell them for their emails, dedicate some time out of your day for social media. Don't just constantly check throughout the day.

I usually spend about 30 minutes each day on social media. That's not to say that I'm necessarily wasting my time on social media. I usually come across some good informational articles and social media keeps me updated on what's going on around the world, friends and colleagues.

7 - Gossiping

Whether you spend too much time reading celebrity tabloids or if you talk about people a lot, spreading gossip can be a huge waste of time.

Not only is it a bad habit but it really has no benefit at all. It won't make you better as a person, it won't earn you money nor will it help anyone else.

STAY AWAY from gossiping.

8 - Taking a long time to get ready

Women are especially guilty of this (some men as well). Many people spend too much time picking out their outfit.

What I usually do is decide on what I'm going to wear the night before.

Pro Tip: When I organize my closet, I usually put together a matching outfit for each hanger, so that every time I decide to change, it takes me a couple minutes top.

Not Having a To-Do List

Every single minute you spend thinking about the tasks you have to do is time wasted. Everyone should have a to-do list, without it, people would feel lost, unorganized, and probably confused about what they have to do.

Spend a couple minutes on your to-do list and that will save you more time over the long haul. Otherwise, you'd spent a lot more time throughout the day just feeling anxious about what you have to do.

CHAPTER 6

BALANCE WORK, LIFE & PLAY

The question of achieving the best work-life balance has been asked throughout history. It is hardly a new concept and employees everywhere continue to debate how best to achieve it.

For millennials, this is a whole other ball park. In an age where smart devices are the norm, and it is possible for most people to work remotely, perhaps the question we should be asking is if the notion of work-life balance is even possible?

That is why in this chapter I will be sharing tips focused on the 20- to 30- somethings navigate the beginning stages of their career without letting health, relationships and happiness fall down the drain.

As we get into a more mobile globalized world, the line between work and play has kind of been blurred in recent years. I am a perfect example of that. I literally work from my laptop. That's how I make money (I will have details on this in another book). Some days I work from home, other days I like getting away and might go to a coffee shop. One time I actually went to a quiet area at the beach under the tree shades, and did my work there.

This all seems amazing to some, and yeah it is quite amazing but the fine line between work and play is not as distinguishable as it once was. Instead of having 9-5's, my work day is within a 24 hour span. The reason why I say this is because sometimes I find myself fiddling through my work tasks late in the evening.

Nearly half of American workers have jobs suitable for part-time or full-time telecommuting (working from outside the office).

Millennials are often looking at job flexibility as one of their key requirements in either accepting or declining a job. Research suggests that millennials place a higher value in being able to spend more time with their family and friends over boomers (when they were younger) who are more keen to work longer hours so that their families can live well off.

I have gathered from my experiences, a few actionable tips on defining the boundaries between work and play.

Pick and Choose

One of the hardest parts of achieving the ultimate work life balance is that we simply cannot choose everything. There is just no way you can attend every gala, go to every dinner party while also working extra-long hours and having home cooked meals every day.

Once you have decided which responsibilities and relationships are the most important to you, all that's left is prioritization.

Follow the 80/20 Rule

Also known as Pareto's Principle, you are probably getting 80% of the results from 20% of the effort. Figure out what that 20% is, and do that 80% of the time.

Be Open to Change

Not every one day will be the same for you. You will have unintended interruptions, whether that may be getting married, having a baby, taking a new job – whatever the situation, be ready to accept the change and adapt accordingly.

Be Yourself

People often try to imitate someone else's lifestyle and come across road blocks that they haven't foreseen. Figure out what's personally meaningful to you, whether that's forming a relationship or working towards a new promotion at your job. As long as you're happy and you have a fulfilling life, it won't matter how drastically different your schedule is from someone else's.

Pursue Your Passions

Just because you're working a lot doesn't necessarily mean your life is dull or boring. Happiness is very subjective and people find content in different things. For some an expensive car is only added stress and misery, for others their passion for cars makes it enjoyable and stress free. Most people in the world live in poverty. I've done quite a few trips across the world and what I saw with my own very eyes were astonishing. Many of these people who barely have a morsel of food for lunch seem the happiest people in the world. The fact that they have food that keeps them going for another day is a blessing in and of itself. Pursue passions that makes you happy and content.

Reconsider Your Commute

Sometimes the physical trip going and coming from work is more draining than the work itself. If standing in a crowded bus or subway makes you sick, consider working closer to home. One of my first jobs required me to commute an hour and a half one way. That was 3 hours wasted of my day. Sure I could have used those 3 hours to read a book or something, but let's be honest here, the commute to work was a placeholder for sleep and the commute back was another placeholder for more sleep.

I can tell you one thing though, once I accepted a job closer to my house I definitely had a better attitude towards work. Of course the opposite can be said about a long commute. If you truly feel happier with a long commute and you know that you can make use of that commute time for something beneficial, then by all means go for it. As I said earlier, do what makes you happy.

Set Up a Physical Barrier

If you're one of those people that work from home for the most part of your job, you need to learn to setup physical boundaries at home. If you have a spare room that isn't being used for anything, use that as your work space. Try to keep all work-related paraphernalia and tasks contained to just this area. One thing I've learned from working for myself and working at home for the most part is **you simply cannot mix your bedroom as your work room.** Things like potentially getting distracted by the pile of dirty laundry on the floor or the TV across your bed will haunt your work life.

Socialize

You need other people that you can do fun stuff with. We are inherently social creatures, and spending all your time alone or with non-social people will take its toll on you.

Make sure you have at least one buddy you can call out of the blue to do something fun, and if you don't have one, find one.

CHAPTER 7

EFFICIENT TIME MANAGEMENT FOR THE SELF-EMPLOYED

I've been self-employed for the last 5 years and one of the reasons why I chose that path was the fact that I knew I would be able to make more money in less time.

One of the benefits of being able to work for yourself is that you have 100% control over most things. This means you set your own hours, you decide how much money you're going to make and you decide when you take your vacation days. The downside to this is the amount of money you make per hour can be lower than a typical 9-5 job.

Self-employed people MUST learn time management otherwise you're not going to be reaching your potential. **The main point of time management in your professional environment is to maximize your earnings by minimizing the time spent.**

Here are some tips that I'd like to share with you all so that you can maximize your potential and earnings with the least amount of time.

Set a Timer

I do this for everything, literally. Virtually any task I do, I set a timer for. The theory behind this is to guestimate how long each task would take. So if one of my tasks is to write a 1000 word blog post on a specified topics, I'd estimate with the SEO research included that it would take me about 20 minutes to write a 500 word blog post. I'd multiply that and would arrive at 40 minutes and add another 5 minutes for unintended interruptions.

I'd set my timer for 45 minutes and this plays a psychological trick on your mind and actually helps you focus even more because you only have one thing on your mind, to finish your task within the allotted time.

Write It Down

Take note of *when you start a task and when you finish* in a small notebook or a smartphone app. I use the 'worklog' app on my android smartphone. This is mainly for logistics purposes and really does help in figuring out how many hours you worked per week, per month.

Create an Outline

When I was still in high school, my English teacher emphasized creating an outline before any work I do almost daily. That thought has stuck to me ever since. Your outline doesn't have to be detailed, simple bullet points is perfect. Once you have a simple outline, you actually save more time by not having to think as much while doing the task.

Work With Dual Monitors

Studies have shown that working with more than one monitor can increase your productivity by as much as 44%. You can hook your laptop up to a second monitor just as easily as a desktop computer. There are even options for tablets.

The 2 Minute Rule

Some productivity experts say that if a tasks take 2 minutes to do, do it as soon as the request comes in. The problem with these small tasks is we humans inherently ignore them till they become big headaches at the end of the week where we have a pile of 100 something tasks that all take 2 minutes to do.

Minimize Meetings

If you're like me, you know that meetings can sometimes be very big time wasters. I'm not saying that meetings aren't important and of course we all need to have meetings to advance our businesses but if you don't need one, try getting out of it. Why? Because sitting in a meeting probably isn't making you much money unless you directly charge people for your time. Communicate by phone, e-mail or messenger app. Building relationships is important, however, so be sensitive to when a meeting might serve that purpose more than productivity.

Delegate as much as you can

If you earn $50/hour, you can afford to pay someone who earns less to do those things you don't quite enjoy doing and aren't the best use of your time. Build a team to take the load off you including help at home. Since most of the work I do is on the internet, I have a couple of VA's (virtual assistant) on my team. Self-employed people have many tedious tasks that they have to do daily and having someone take that load off you cannot just save you so much time, but can also make you even more money.

If you're wondering where you can also hire a VA, I usually go on Upwork (formerly ODesk). Most of my VA's are from the Philippines and the rate at which I hire is very reasonable.

Work Smarter, Not Harder

Some people will proclaim that they have 16 hour work days. The question is, how much of those 16 hours is actual work done. Yes, as entrepreneurs and self-employed people, we kind of have to be available throughout the day but research suggests once a person reaches about 40 hours in a week, any time beyond that is usually less productive.

Learn how to maximize what you do in the least amount of time as I have mentioned how to do with the previous tips.

CHAPTER 8

THE IMPORTANCE OF A NIGHT TIME ROUTINE

How you feel during your waking hours is greatly dependent on how well you slept the night before. Your sleep schedule, bedtime habits, and day-to-day lifestyle choices can make an enormous difference to the quality of your nightly rest.

Almost all the mega-successful people you know all have a night time routine they stick by, and that is precisely why they can afford to be so successful. Creating rituals is one of the most powerful ways to effect a change in behavior, as over time these healthy habits will become automatic so you don't have to think about them. Not only do you have better quality sleep, but you also wake up with more energy to do the things that are important to you.

I've developed my own night time routine a couple of years ago and have stuck to it ever since. Everyone's routine will cater to their respective needs so find what works for you.

These routines don't have to boring, in fact they can be extremely enjoyable. Here are some tips to help you develop an effective night time routine.

Assess Your Day

Ben Franklin one of the founding fathers of the USA was known for his rigorous schedules and routines. He use to ask himself every night before he went to bed "What good did I do today?"

Additionally, you can ask yourself...

- What progress did I make towards my vision and goals?

- What am I grateful for today?
- What improvements can I make with what I learned today?

I ask myself these questions every night and have always felt a sense of motivation gushing through my soul. If my day wasn't as productive as I would have liked it to be, I would theorized what the bottlenecks were and I would've taken steps to make sure that the next day was more productive.

Read for 30 Minutes to an Hour

Former Microsoft CEO Bill Gates is an avid reader and he makes that public. Each night before going to sleep he reads a book, ranging on topics from politics to current events. Aside from the obvious benefit of learning new information, reading also helps with stress reduction and improves your memory and cognitive abilities. A 2009 study from the University of Essex revealed that reading for as little as six minutes a day can reduce stress levels by up to 68%.

Pro Tip: If you have a kindle device, I highly suggest you sign up for Kindle Unlimited. You pay a monthly fee of $9.99 and borrow up to 10 books at a time.

Unplug

Unplugging is also a key to a good night's sleep. In the past before we had the technology we have today, and even before we had electricity, people use to sleep when it was dark and wake up during the earlier portion of the day along with the sunrise. This has changed drastically with the advent of technology and artificial light.

According to Dr Charles Czeisler, a professor of sleep medicine at Harvard University, the bright lights produced by our cell phone screens disrupt our bodies natural sleep rhythm and actually "trick" our bodies into thinking it's daytime. Those bright lights send a message to our brains that prevents certain chemicals from being released, causing us to have a much harder time going to sleep.

Pro Tip: No TV, Internet, Phone, Movies, Tablets.

Consistent Sleep Schedule

Once you have found your optimal sleep time, don't change it. It is important that your body and mind adapt to a certain sleep time. This will turn into habit later which will make it much easier for you to go to bed distraction free.

Hygiene

Having the right hygiene will make it easier to sleep and is good in general.

Here are the steps I take every night.

- Floss every single teeth, don't let any residue remain or else it'll be a problem later.
- Brush my teeth for 5-8 minutes.
- Wash my face with cold water
- Drink 2-3 glasses of water
- Unplug from all the electronics
- Read a book for 30 minutes
- Turn off the lights completely
- SLEEP

Meditation

This is one of those tips that not many people do. There's often times a stigma surrounding meditation, and there has always been a debate as to whether mediation is actually helpful. But when a 2014 study took a look at over 19,000 cases involving mediation, the results were clear. Meditation was found to help reduce stress, anxiety, depression, and pain. So regardless of one's view of mediation, you can't argue with the results.

I quite love doing this as it eases my mind and gives me a sense of purpose. Meditation can lower cortisol and adrenaline levels.

Here are the steps I take in my meditation before bed.

1 – Take 5 deep breaths. As you breathe out, imagine the thoughts and feelings of the day just disappearing into the distance, and any feelings of tension in the body just melting away.

2 – While lying in bed, try placing your hands on your belly. "When you breathe in and breathe out, your hands may gently move," says Kathy Doner, MD, who has a full-time hypnotherapy practice in Sebastian, Fla. "Focusing on this movement gets your mind off of your busy thoughts and onto your body. You can distract yourself and bring yourself to a different place. It's very calming."

3 – I like to imagine my life 5 years into the future and see how much of an improvement I've become over my younger self.

When all is said and done, trust me when I say this, you will feel so good that you wish it wouldn't end. You will definitely wake up with more motivation and purpose and ready to get down to business.

CHAPTER 9

BENEFITS OF WAKING UP EARLY

When was the last time you could honestly say that you had the best A.M ever, for most people the answer would probably have been 'never'. And to be quite honest, mornings can be very exhausting, tiring and hectic and the only thing going through your head is how you can go back to bed.

A 2012 study published in an American Psychological Association journal, Emotion. Among the 700 adults asked about their emotional state, health and preferred time of day, self-professed "morning people" reported feeling happier and healthier than night owls.

Not only is that scientifically backed up, but from personal experience I've never been a morning person. If you go a couple of chapters up I tell you how my life was without a good morning schedule, it was awful! I can now say that I'm a self-professed "morning person" and life couldn't have been better.

How do you start off your morning? Whatever the case may be, what you do in the morning sets your mood for the rest of the day. It makes sense, then, to make sure you're having the healthiest, most productive morning possible.

When you look at majorly successful people such as the POTUS Barrack Obama, Mark Zuckerberg, Bill Gates you often wonder, with them ruling the country and owning billions of dollars, they must do a lot to reach that state. How do they have enough time for it all? Well for starters, all of them are well known morning rise and shiners.

"Early to bed and early to rise makes a man healthy, wealthy and wise" – *Ben Franklin, famously*

What Got Me Motivated to Wake Up Early?

I've read countless articles and books on the benefits of waking up early and the state of happiness one reaches by doing so, but I never really thought I would ever do it just because of the said level of difficulty for most people. Especially for me, where my usual wake up time was around 11am.

Then one summer my sleep time was really messed up. I would find my-self on my phone late at night typing away, checking every social media post, watching movies until I found myself awake at 4:30am. This became a habit of mine for 2-3 months and had a major effect on my life. I would find myself waking up around 3 pm where pretty much my whole day went by in the flash of an eye, I started going to the gym a lot less, and my physical activity was almost nil. I started eating a lot more and gained a lot of weight. I got very dark eye bags which to this day still have not left me (even after all this with good health and rest). 'Depression' is the only term I can put it in simply. This is when it hit me, how much more of this can I take. That's when I started to make small and subtle changes that would ultimately help me get out of this dilemma.

Before anything, I started reading on the benefits of waking up early again, but this time with passion and excitement. I really wanted to make a change, and what better way to do it then to motivate myself.

According to studies, yes. There are actual recognizable benefits to waking up early.

Early birds, rejoice!

Becoming and Early Riser Will Make You More Successful

Sounds cliché doesn't it, but there is some truth to it and some science to back it up. A 2008 study out of Texas University concluded that those students identifying themselves as early birds earned a full point higher on their GPAs than those who identified themselves as night owls.

Better Quality Sleep

Contrary to popular belief, the quantity of sleep doesn't matter as much as the quality of sleep. 6 hours of quality sleep is more preferable to 9 hours of sleep that still leaves you tired and drowsy.

Once you hit a consistent sleep schedule and wake up at a certain time every day, your body will adjust and not only will it be easier for you to rise in the morning, you will also feel tired at night and fall asleep faster.

Get a Head Start

When you're consistently waking up at 6am, you are awake when 99% of your 'time zone' is asleep. Not only does this create a feel-good factor, it increases productivity.

During this time you can focus on your most important tasks and get them over with. The rest of the day will feel like a breeze and not stressful.

Increased Productivity

On the days I'm awake extremely early, the productivity soars through the roof. It's a benefit that comes from getting a head start. The head start creates a motivation to continue your lead ahead, resulting in (a) more things getting completed (b) things getting completed faster.

A recent study by Christopher Randler, a biology professor at the University of Education at Heidelberg, surveyed 367 university students, asking them when they were the most energetic and willing to change a situation. According to the study, morning people were more likely to agree with statements such as "I feel in charge of making things happen."

Less Stress (Major Key)

Everyone has those days where they wake up just an hour before their work time, without properly brushing their teeth, they rush into their unfinished breakfast, and poorly dress themselves. The whole time, they are in a state of constant stress and by the time they get to work, their mind isn't having it. The motivation to work isn't there and the only they want to do is go home rest/sleep.

Exercise

One of things I tell my coaching clients when I help them with their morning routine is to exercise in the morning. Waking up early is already manifested happiness, but exercising in the morning takes that to the next level.

You have higher levels of energy, more blood flowing in your system and there is more motivation to get things done.

CHAPTER 10

5 GUARANTEED WAYS TO DESTROY YOUR MORNING ROUTINE

In the last chapter we talked about the benefits of waking up early, but in this chapter we're taking a 360 turn. Yeah early mornings are great but ONLY if done the correct way. There are just some things that can ruin it for you and you must be aware of them if you want to avoid them.

I've been blabbering on and on about how my life is great with a good morning routine, but I too have those days where things just aren't going right.

I've done every single one of these mistakes at least once in the past and I still do time to time when I can't help it. But the days I avoid these mistakes altogether are the days I'm at the zenith of my productivity.

You Snooze You Lose

I know for a fact I'm not the first one to tell you to avoid the snooze button, and there is a reason people will always tell you to avoid it. It honestly does nothing more than waste time. That extra 10 minutes of sleep that you get does more harm than good and believe it or not, it will actually make you feel even more tired due to not giving your body adequate time.

To this day, I will still hit the snooze button from time to time. After having a much stronger discipline currently, I probably have that to about 2 days out of a month. It's going to be hard, and it's going to take a while to master, but you have to start off by telling yourself you must wake up at a certain time. With enough time, it will become a habit and the snooze button will be a thing of the past.

Skipping Breakfast

Seriously, just stop missing breakfast or having a half assed breakfast. Breakfast kick-starts your metabolism, helping you burn calories throughout the day. It also gives you the energy you need to get things done and helps you focus at work or at school. Those are just a few reasons why it's the most important meal of the day.

Many studies have linked eating breakfast to good health, including better memory and concentration, lower levels of "bad" LDL cholesterol, and lower chances of getting diabetes, heart disease, and being overweight.

I can't begin to tell you how much of an effect, having a full and healthy breakfast will do to you.

Not Drinking Enough Water

It is a well-known fact that drinking water first thing in the morning before any solid food is digested purifies your internal system. If you have enough fluids in the morning, not only will you feel happier, sharper, and more energetic, but you'll also have more strength, speed, and stamina for your workouts later.

- Water will keep you hydrated and your skin very smooth with a slight tint of glow throughout the day.
- Drinking water first thing in the morning increases the rate at which new muscle and blood cells are produced.
- When you consume about 16 ounces of water (chilled), you will boost your body's metabolism by about 24% thus help you lose those extra pounds.

I usually have about 4 glasses of water first thing in the morning and to be very honest, my days always seemed better on days I drank more water.

Get Natural Sunlight (THIS MEANS NO CELLPHONES)

Firstly, exposure to 20 to 30 minutes of natural light in the morning hours helps set your internal clock and regulate your energy level, appetite, and metabolism, according to researchers.

Secondly, no matter how much you want to keep away from your smart devices till you have done all your essential needs. Don't wake up and check your emails or social media first thing in the morning, for everyone's sake.

Cramming

If you want to start your day with the worst possible mood, please go ahead and cram everything. By all means, wake up as late as you can, skip your breakfast and water/milk, rush to the subway and arrive 10 minutes late.

That is what you call a formula for disaster. Cramming will not do you any good, and if you've learned anything from this book is that you want to have enough time to do the things that are important to you.

CHAPTER 11

HEALTH, FITNESS AND ENERGY

Physical activity improves quality of life, there I said it. It's not hard to digest. If I ask you if you'd like to…

- Decrease your risk of disease
- Feel better physically and mentally
- Have more energy throughout the day
- Look better
- Help avoid injuries

What answer would you give me?

Regular physical exercise can reduce and prevent many diseases and improve physical and mental health. It can even help you live longer, like who doesn't want to live longer and healthier.

Exercise Controls Weight

Regular exercise can help prevent excess weight gain or help maintain weight loss. How you ask? Simply put, whenever you are doing any form of physical exercise, you are burning off calories, the more calories you burn off, the greater the weight loss assuming you have proper diet.

If you don't have time or whatever else excuse you could think of, you can do incorporate exercise into your daily habits. Instead of taking the elevators, why not take the stairs. Instead of walking to a certain place, why not bike it.

Exercise Combats Health Conditions and Diseases

Worried about heart disease? Hoping to prevent high blood pressure? No matter what your current weight, being active boosts high-density lipoprotein (HDL), or "good," cholesterol and decreases unhealthy triglycerides. This one-two punch keeps your blood flowing smoothly, which decreases your risk of cardiovascular diseases.

Exercise Improves Mood

I'll tell you from personal experience, I'm always happier after a good workout. Yeah my body might be aching throughout, and yeah I might have a tough time walking after it but boy does that pain give you a major sense of accomplishment. Exercise is also a great way to blow off steam. I know many people including some near and dear friends who resort to drugs to blow off steam. Temporary relief was never the answer and it never will.

Physical activity stimulates various brain chemicals that may leave you feeling happier and more relaxed. You may also feel better about your appearance and yourself when you exercise regularly, which can boost your confidence and improve your self-esteem.

Now let's flip the question around and ask, what happens without any physical activity in your life?

Well for starters…

- Increased risks of anxiety, stress, and feelings of depression
- high blood pressure, coronary heart diseases, diabetes, osteoporosis, colon cancer, and obesity

Yeah, I definitely don't want to be in the latter category. Now that we got the reasons out of the way, how do we get started?

It's very easy to get started, and seriously, all you have to do is tell yourself that you need to get started right now. Crazy how the mind works right! Hey, talking to yourself doesn't mean you're crazy.

According to psychologist Linda Sapadin, talking out loud to yourself helps you validate important and difficult decisions. *"It helps you clarify your thoughts, tend to what's important and firm up any decisions you're contemplating."*

But on a more practical note, The American Heart Association recommends at least 150-minutes of moderate activity each week. An easy way to remember this is 30 minutes at least 5 days a week, but three 10-minute periods of activity are as beneficial to your overall fitness as one 30-minute session. This is achievable! Physical activity may also help encourage you to spend some time outdoors.

CHAPTER 12

37 PRODUCTIVITY TIPS THAT WILL BOOST YOUR DAY

I didn't want to end off without giving y'all some real good food for thought. This is going to be an exhaustive list and for the most part self-explanatory. Without further ado…

1 – **Love what you do.** Enjoying tasks will make you work that much harder.

2 – **Set a timer** for each of your tasks.

3 – **Take a break.** Productivity will never remain at 100% utilization ever. You have to take breaks to recharge.

4 – **Declutter your desk.** Productivity and cluttered spaces don't match well.

5 – **Be part of the 20%.** This means even if you squander the 80% of work by not being productive, take about 20% of 'your work day and try utilizing the time to a near 90%.

6 – **Work less.** Think you can get more done by tacking on extra hours? According to a 2014 study by Stanford professor John Pencavel, who examined data from laborers during World War I, output was proportionate to time worked—up to 49 hours. Beyond that, it rose at a decreasing rate, and those who put in 70 hours had the same productivity as someone who worked 56 hours.

7 – **Plan each day the night before.** If you spend just 15 minutes before you go to bed the night before, you will have a head start on your day when the morning rolls around.

8 – **Complete the tasks you hate most to do first thing In the morning.** You know if you dread a task, you will most likely end up procrastinating on it.

9 – **Just do it.** This Nike slogan never fails to amaze me. Honestly people, all you have to do is take the first step and it's a roller coaster ride from there.

10 – **Write a blog to document your own personal achievements and goals.** I do this too. It helps very much in keeping you in line with your goals and holds you accountable.

11 – **Step away from the computer.** Although the computer can be an amazing productivity tool, sometimes you just have to take a step back because of all the distractions it comes with.

12 – **Get plenty of sleep.** I've mentioned so many times in this book how important this is. The more quality sleep, the more productive you will be.

13 – **Drink lots of water.** It's very important to stay hydrated throughout the day. There are many benefits as I have talked about in the previous chapters.

14 – **Exercise.** Research suggests that midday exercises actually help you in boosting your productivity.

15 – **Outsource as much as possible.** I outsource almost all my simple but dreaded tasks. You'd think I'm losing money because of this but on the contrary, I'm making even more money.

16 – **Turn off the TV.** Or better yet, throw it out completely.

17 – **Read books, lots of them.** I read as much as I can. I feel smarter every day. I feel like I can do more things every day. Your stomach isn't the only thing that needs food.

18 – **Listen to educational audio books.** If you're finding it difficult to read books/ebooks, why not try out audio books. Sometimes I find myself listening to these when I'm in my commute.

19 – **Auto pay your bills.** If you have lots of bills then you know this will save you lots of time.

20 – **Take shorter showers.** Hey I'm not saying I don't take longer showers either but it's true to say you will save a lot of time with shorter showers.

21 – **Tell other people about your goals.** When you know someone is watching your moves, then you're more inclined to commit to that goal. I've found myself failing many goals and my friends would sometimes bring up about how I fail on goals more than them.

22 – **Learn to say NO.** We simply cannot do everything and must learn to prioritize some things over others.

23 – **Find a mentor.** Whether you have to pay that person or give something in return. Your return on investment will be 10x folds.

24 – **Find a coach.** Whenever I decided to start a new business venture, the first thing I do is find a coach. It saves me lots of time and money over the long haul.

25 – **Set exciting goals.** The more exciting the goal is, the more you will enjoy achieving it.

26 – **Reward yourself for finishing a task.** The truth is, motivation dies out very quickly. Rewarding yourself is a great way of keeping that fire lit.

27 – **Shop online.** Aside from the general purchases like groceries, I shop mostly online. Especially with Amazon Prime and their same day or 2 day shipping, it saves a lot of time going to the store and looking for items.

28 – **Improve your typing speed.** I write every morning, and every day I'm constantly improving ever so slightly on my typing speed. Trust me on this, you will save a lot of time this way.

29 – **When reading a book, read the parts that you need and skip the rest.** I wouldn't generally advise this as I like reading wholly, but the reality of the matter is, most books have filler sections and added words that take away from learning what you need faster.

30 – **Cook your meals in bulk.**

31 – **Learn to speed read.**

32 – **Look at something nice.** It may sound unlikely, but some research shows outfitting an office with aesthetically pleasing elements--like plants--can increase productivity by up to 15 percent. Jazz up your office space with pictures, candles, flowers, or anything else that puts a smile on your face.

33 – **Turn off notifications for a certain time frame.** No one can be expected to resist the allure of an email, voicemail, or text notification.

34 – **Take advantage of your commute.** People spend on average about 1.5-2.5 hours commuting each and every day. Imagine what you can do with that time. If you're on the bus read a

book. If you're walking you can download and listen to a podcast, or an audiobook.

35 – **Stop multitasking.** Just stop it.

36 - **Track and limit how much time you're spending on tasks.** Once you've tracked enough of the time you spend on tasks, you will have enough information on how long each task should take.

37 – **Get broadband internet connection.** Slow internet is not something you want in this day and age.

There you have it folks. My exhaustive list productivity tips that will boost your day. I think I just shed a tear.

CHAPTER 13

9 AWESOME TIME MANAGEMENT TOOLS YOU SHOULD CONSIDER

I hope you've enjoyed reading this book thus far. As we near the end, I am going to share with you some of the tools that I use to facilitate productivity and effective time management.

These tools have helped me a lot in my journey. I've stopped using some as my time management skills get better and I have less need for these tools, but as someone beginning to change their habits and optimize their time, these tools are definitely something you should check out.

RescueTime

This is definitely one of my most favorite time tracking application. Many time management tools also endorse this application as they have seen results from using this tool.

It tracks how you use your computer, from soup to nuts. It tracks what websites you use, and then breaks them into categories for more in-depth look. You can block yourself from distracting websites, and even set manual timers away from the computer.

Capture Everything in One Place

Dropbox

You've all heard of this one. There are many competitors out there in the file sharing/cloud storage business including big names such as Google and Apple. Dropbox has been there for a very long time and have continuously tweaked their product to make it one of the best.

Evernote

Evernote is a free productivity tool that allows you to capture all your ideas, thoughts and images in many different ways, eg with voice, notes or images.

Need to Get Something Done Without Distractions?

Focus Booster

This app is based on the principles of the pomodoro technique for individuals who procrastinate and feel overwhelmed by tasks. It is designed to enhance your focus and remove any anxiety you might have with time.

Tools to Track Time Spent on Projects

Toggl

Let me be clear, and as I have said many times before, effective time management first starts with tracking your time in order to analyze and optimize it. Toggl is a great free tool that I use to do just that.

Work Log Android App

This is a very simple time log tracking app. You punch in when you start working, and you punch out when you're done.

Mind Mapping Tools

MindMeister

Mind mapping is a great way to build focus without distractions. It gives you a sense of purpose and motivation which is always a good thing. They have an app as well along with their online application.

Mind42

This is another great free mind mapping tool. I haven't used it personally but have heard great things about it.

Do You Ever Forget Your Passwords?

Universal Password Manager

This tool allows you to keep all your passwords locked away in an encrypted database and you can access these passwords with one password. This saves a lot of time especially when you always end up clicking "*forgot password.*"

Remove Distractions Surfing the Web

Pocketfree

This is a great tool that makes it easy to read articles without the added distractions of excess advertisements and such. You can save any article to read it later.

This list isn't exhaustive by any means and most of the aforementioned applications I have used myself.

Now you can me a time master as well ☺

CONCLUSION

Here comes the sad part. It's honestly been a fun writing this for you guys and I hope you enjoyed the rollercoaster ride.

We are heading into unchartered territory where once people had so much time on their hand before the advent of advanced technology, whereas now we can barely spare a few minutes for what we love.

Technology can be a good thing, or it can be bad. It truly depends on who uses it and what they use it for.

I've shared with you almost everything I know and have done with regards to managing your time. I've shared with you some of my own experiences.

Now it's your time to build new experiences. Now it's your time to make enough time to spend with your family, or go on a 2 month long vacation around the world without time anxiety.

No one said it was going to be easy, but it definitely beats the hell out of having to do everything under time pressure.

Go out there, enjoy what life has to give and own the world!

Peace!

CAN I ASK A FAVOUR?

If you enjoyed this book, found it useful or otherwise then I'd really appreciate it if you would post a short review on Amazon. I do read all the reviews personally so that I can continually write what people are wanting.

If you'd like to leave a review then please head over to Amazon.

Thank you for your support!

About The Author

Mohammed Khan is a writer, author, entrepreneur, life coach, personal trainer, speaker and an avid traveler.

Mohammed has been making money online since 2013 and decided to hop on to Kindle and share with the world his wealth of knowledge. Mohammed loves the luxury of being able to travel and yet make money doing so.

He always tells his clients, you don't need to think of travelling as an expense but rather as an investment.

Some of his hobbies include:

- Meditation, Mindfulness and The Meaning of Life
- Running, Biking, Swimming, Rock Climbing
- Helping Individuals Reach Their Full Potential
- Spending Time With His Family
- Playing Competitive Basketball
- Writing, Traveling, Blogging

If you want to learn more about Mohammed or how to earn income online, you can go ahead and visit his blog.

www.ingramcontent.com/pod-product-compliance
Lightning Source LLC
Chambersburg PA
CBHW070359190526
45169CB00003B/1050